C<u>ONTENTS</u>

Series editor: Tim Carr

BIBLE SOCIETY
Stonehill Green, Westlea, SWINDON SN5 7DG, England

First published 1991

British Library Cataloguing in Publication Data
Keay, Kathy
    Women at Home
    1. Bible. Special subjects. Society. Role of women
    I. Title   II. Bible Society   III. Series
    220.830542

ISBN 0–564–05965X

Printed in Great Britain by Stanley L. Hunt (Printers) Ltd,
Rushden, Northants

Bible Societies exist to provide resources for Bible distribution and use.
Bible Society in England and Wales (BFBS) is a member of the United
Bible Societies, an international partnership working in over 180
countries. Their common aim is to reach all people with the Bible, or
some part of it, in a language they can understand and at a price they can
afford. Parts of the Bible have now been translated into approximately
1900 languages. Bible Societies aim to help every church at every point
where it uses the Bible. You are invited to share in this work by your
prayers and gifts. The Bible Society in your country will be very happy to
provide details of its activity.

INTRODUCTION

"Home Sweet Home." Is this how women today feel about their homes? Once home was a place within the community where work, recreation and family relationships could thrive. Yet for many thousands of people today it has become little more than a temporary resting place, where husband and children look to mum to service them and where professional women turn around in between work and "evenings out".

The traditional pattern where men go out to work and women stay at home has not surprisingly been strongly challenged in recent years by both the women's movement and economic factors. There has been a strong reaction to this, not least within the Church, from those who see these changing social patterns as a threat to family life.

While different groups hold different views, in reality life is harsh, and there is often no choice as to what path to take. For example, single women and female heads of households usually have to support themselves financially, which in most cases means finding work outside the home for large parts of the day, and long periods of their lives.

In spite of the difficulties working outside the home often involves, women who do so are often envied by those who have been made to feel second rate because they are "only" housewives. A good number of these women long to find a job or establish a career outside the home. However, the results of the present "enterprise culture" in Britain and the availability of home computers are seeing more and more women opting for a more flexible lifestyle where they can work on a self-employed basis from home.

† How true is it that life and fulfilment are to be found by and large outside the home?

1

† Are we moving towards a lifestyle which encourages women and men alike to develop different parts of their life and work more fully than before?

The aim of these studies is to explore what the Bible has to say on the subject of "home" and "homelessness". In doing this women and men are able to get a renewed sense of "home", and this in turn can help develop new ways of approaching work and community life which make practical sense in their everyday lives.

USING SYMBOLS IN THE GROUP STUDIES

After the Bible passages you will see the following symbols:

 something you have learned about God

 something you have learned about yourself or human nature

 a new insight

 something to put into practice

 something to do together

Re-read the passage, and then apply the symbols to what you have read.

If you are not going to write in this booklet, keep a note-book to record what you have gained from each study. Bring one with you before the first session. At the start of each new session, write the Bible passage at the top of a new page. Date it so that you can look back and see what you have learned.

Here is an example:

Session One – Mary and Martha

 Spending time in God's presence is important (Luke 10.42)

 Don't be over-anxious about material things (Matthew 6.25)

 God cares for me and knows all my needs (Matthew 6.26)

 Plan to spend more time in listening to him and studying his word. Work out what stops me doing this.

 Talk to others in the group about how much time we spend on different things.

SESSION ONE

THE HOME OF MARY AND MARTHA: A PLACE FOR MAKING CHOICES

"The mass media usually portray the homemaker as the helpless, sometimes giddy woman whose major concerns in life revolve about her embarrassed husband's ring around the collar, her dull floors, cooking for the family, and buying the right toilet paper." *Bobbye D. Sorrels*

AIM

To look at how we spend time in our homes, and the challenges and the choices we face.

TO TALK ABOUT

"A woman's place is in the home."

† Do you agree? Turn to the person next to you and talk about it for 3 minutes. Now give the other person a turn to express his or her views.
† What are the main points that have emerged? Note them down.
† How does the way women are portrayed affect your self-image and the way in which you view work and your home?

5

"Above all, home is a place to be ourselves." *Barbara Smith*

† This can mean a place of rest and a place of self-contradiction, where anxieties are aired and important choices made about our lives from day to day. How is this true in your life?

You may want to write down a few thoughts in a notebook, and refer back to it as you go through these studies.

MAKING CHOICES

The first Bible passage is part of the account of Jesus' journey to Jerusalem. On the way he stopped off at the home of two sisters, Mary and Martha. His encounter with them challenged and affirmed both women. Remember that this was in a society which had a low and restricted view of women, and where most were expected to be married and to have children. Read the passage now.

[38]As Jesus and his disciples went on their way, he came to a village where a woman named Martha welcomed him in her home. [39]She had a sister named Mary, who sat down at the feet of the Lord and listened to his teaching. [40]Martha was upset over all the work she had to do, so she came and said, "Lord, don't you care that my sister has left me to do all the work by myself? Tell her to come and help me!"

[41]The Lord answered her, "Martha, Martha! You are worried and troubled over so many things, [42]but just one is needed. Mary has chosen the right thing, and it will not be taken away from her."
Luke 10.38–42

Re-read the passage, and apply the symbols to what you have read.

 something you have learned about God

something you have learned about yourself or
human nature

 a new insight

 something to put into practice

 something to do together

DIGGING DEEPER

† How do you interpret this story? Do you think Martha
gets a raw deal, or would she usually choose to take
control on the domestic front even when guests are not
around?

† Is Martha using this situation to make the point that
Mary should help more around the house, or is she simply feeling left out?

† What does Jesus say to Martha and to women in the
home who are "preoccupied with many things"?

† What is the "one thing" that Mary has chosen? Why does
Jesus say that it will not be taken away from her?
What is Jesus saying here about a woman's ability to
choose what she sees as most important in life?

† Do we support women in the different choices they make
and the different lifestyles they lead, or expect them to
conform to one model?

† Imagine the Mary and Martha household when Jesus is
not there. How could things change for the better for
both women?

† What lessons do we learn from this passage about our
own roles within our homes?

7

Now read this passage:

²⁵"This is why I tell you not to be worried about the food and drink you need in order to stay alive, or about clothes for your body. After all, isn't life worth more than food? And isn't the body worth more than clothes? ²⁶Look at the birds: they do not sow seeds, gather a harvest and put it in barns; yet your Father in heaven takes care of them! Aren't you worth much more than birds? ²⁷Can any of you live a bit longer by worrying about it? ³³Instead, be concerned above everything else with the Kingdom of God and with what he requires of you, and he will provide you with all these other things."

Matthew 6.25–27, 33

REFLECTION

Think about your own life. How much time and energy do you take up buying food and clothes?

On the circle on page 9 show how you spend your time, and what priorities you give to each activity, inside and outside your home.

For example:

h = in the home
o = outside the home

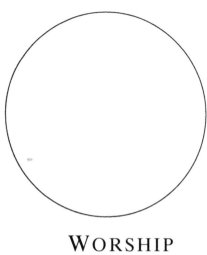

WORSHIP

Write a prayer or meditation thanking God for your home and all that goes on in it. Be honest about areas that still need to be resolved in your life and in your home.

SESSION TWO

THE WIDOW AT ZAREPHATH: A PLACE OFFERING HOSPITALITY AND SHELTER

"Is anyone there?"
"Will someone let me in?"
"Our world is full of strangers. In it we experience a painful search for a hospitable place, where life can be lived without fear. We need to know that there is someone at home in the universe who will take us in, welcome us and make us feel safe." *Henri Nouwen*

AIM

To re-examine our homes as places offering hospitality and shelter, and also our link with the community in which we live.

TO TALK ABOUT

Sometimes hospitality is given and received in the most unlikely places, and often by women who are on their own. In a world which is made for couples, women who live alone have often been made to feel grateful and even socially "odd" by those who try to include them within their own family circle. Yet those who know what it's like to feel an outsider can become those who are best known for offering hospitality and shelter to others.

† Take a moment to think of women you know. Is this true of anyone in particular?

† Turn to the person next to you and talk about how you have been welcomed into the home of someone who didn't know you. What impressed you most about that person?

HOSPITALITY AND SHELTER

Read the following passage from 1 Kings. It tells how the prophet Elijah was sent by God to a widow in the village of Zarephath, and how through her he was miraculously fed from the little that she had. Remember that this was at a time when widows really had nothing much to live on – long before the days of the pension!

[7]After a while the brook dried up because of the lack of rain. [8]Then the LORD said to Elijah, [9]"Now go to the town of Zarephath, near Sidon, and stay there. I have commanded a widow who lives there to feed you." [10]So Elijah went to Zarephath, and as he came to the gate of the town, he saw a widow gathering firewood. "Please bring me a drink of water," he said to her. [11]And as she was going to get it, he called out, "And please bring me some bread, too."

[12]She answered, "By the living LORD your God I swear that I haven't got any bread. All I have is a handful of flour in a bowl and a drop of olive-oil in a jar. I came here to gather some firewood to take back home and prepare what little I have for my son and me. That will be our last meal, and then we will starve to death."

[13]"Don't worry," Elijah said to her. "Go ahead and prepare your meal. But first make a small loaf from what you have and bring it to me, and then prepare the rest for you and your son. [14]For this is what the LORD the God of Israel, says: 'The bowl will not run out of flour or the jar run out of oil before the day that I, the LORD, send rain.'"

[15]The widow went and did as Elijah had told her, and all of them had enough food for many days. [16]As the LORD had promised through Elijah, the bowl did not run out of flour nor did the jar run out of oil.

1 Kings 17.7–16

11

Re-read the passage and apply the symbols to what you have read.

 something you have learned about God

 something you have learned about yourself or human nature

 a new insight

 something to put into practice

 something to do together

DIGGING DEEPER

† Why do you think Elijah asked for the widow's last bit of meal and oil?

† What do you think is the main point of this story?

Now read this passage:

⁹As the scripture says,
"He gives generously to the needy;
his kindness lasts for ever."
¹⁰And God, who supplies seed to sow and bread to eat, will also supply you with all the seed you need and will make it grow and pro-duce a rich harvest from your generosity. ¹¹He will always make you rich enough to be generous at all times, so that many will thank God for your gifts which they receive from us.
2 Corinthians 9.8–11

REFLECTION

† Has this always been true in your experience?

† Take a moment to think of people you know who would

like to be invited to your house, perhaps for a meal. Make a short list. Look in your diary and see if you can invite one or two people a month on a regular basis. Commit these times to God and ask him to bring something really special out of them. Keep a diary of what happens.

WORSHIP

"The biggest disease today is not leprosy or tuberculosis, but the feeling of being unwanted, uncared for and deserted by everybody."

"Our biggest problem today is not hunger, but loneliness." *Mother Teresa*

Lord, forgive me for the times when selfishly, I fill my own stomach and enjoy the company of those who share my home, forgetting those who have no home, little food and no one close to them to love. Help me to realize that in welcoming those who need warmth and friendship, I am welcoming you. Amen.

SESSION THREE

THE HOME OF RAHAB THE PROSTITUTE: A HIDING PLACE

"Let us always remain children, ever on the threshold of old age – loaded with real adventures." *Paul Tournier*

AIM

To see how our homes can be places of refuge and shelter, and how they can be used for God's work.

TO TALK ABOUT

This study shows how a woman's home can become an important place of refuge and shelter. In this passage a prostitute uses her home as a hiding place for two spies. In every generation, there have been women whose otherwise ordinary lives have been transformed as they have offered up their homes for bigger causes than their own.

[1]*Then Joshua sent two spies from the camp at Acacia with orders to go and secretly explore the land of Canaan, especially the city of Jericho. When they came to the city, they went to spend the night in the house of a prostitute named Rahab. [2]The king of Jericho heard that* some Israelites had come that night to spy out the country, [3]*so he sent word to Rahab: "The men in your house have come to spy out the whole country! Bring them out!"*
[4-6]*"Some men did come to my house," she answered, "but I don't know where they were from. They*

left at sunset before the city gate was closed. I didn't find out where they were going, but if you start after them quickly, you can catch them." (Now Rahab had taken the two spies up on the roof and hidden them under some stalks of flax that she had put there.) ⁷The king's men left the city, and then the gate was shut. They went looking for the Israelite spies as far as the place where the road crosses the Jordan.

⁸Before the spies settled down for the night, Rahab went up on the roof ⁹and said to them, "I know that the LORD has given you this land. Everyone in the country is terrified of you. ¹⁰We have heard how the LORD dried up the Red Sea in front of you when you were leaving Egypt. We have also heard how you killed Sihon and Og, the two Amorite kings east of the Jordan. ¹¹We were afraid as soon as we heard about it; we have all lost our courage because of you. The LORD your God is God in heaven above and here on earth. ¹²Now swear by him that you will treat my family as kindly as I have treated you, and give me some sign that I can trust you. ¹³Promise me that you will save my father and mother, my brothers and sisters, and all their families! Don't let us be killed!"

¹⁴The men said to her, "May God take our lives if we don't do as we say! If you do not tell anyone what we have been doing, we promise you that when the LORD gives us this land, we will treat you well."

¹⁵Rahab lived in a house built into the city wall, so she let the men down from the window by a rope. ¹⁶"Go into the hill-country," she said, "or the king's men will find you. Hide there for three days until they come back. After that you can go on your way."

Joshua 2.1–16

Read the following story:

In a crooked little Dutch house, one room wide, Corrie Ten Boom lived a fairly uneventful life for fifty-five years. She was a single woman who was a watchmaker and also cared for her older sister and elderly father. She had no idea what lay round the corner for her family and for their home. As the Nazis swept through Europe, their small house became a hiding place for local Jews, and a place where visitors could always be guaranteed real coffee, even in the middle of the war.

† List ways in which those who have homes of their own

15

could use them from time to time to help those who need a place of refuge and shelter, at home and overseas.

A HIDING PLACE

The book of Joshua records how Joshua led the people of Israel into the land which God had promised them. The first five chapters focus on their entry into Canaan. Spies were sent out to view the land. Crossing the Jordan and capturing Jericho were key to the whole campaign. This passage tells the story of how Rahab the prostitute saved herself and her family by hiding the spies in her house, once the king of Jericho had heard that they were in the city.

Re-read the passage, and apply the symbols to what you have read.

 something you have learned about God

 something you have learned about yourself or human nature

 a new insight

 something to put into practice

 something to do together

Now read the following passage:

[1]To have faith is to be sure of the things we hope for, to be certain of the things we cannot see.
[31]It was faith that kept the prostitute Rahab from being killed with those who disobeyed God, for she gave the Israelite spies a friendly welcome.

Hebrews 11.1, 31

DIGGING DEEPER

Rahab is one of only two women mentioned with all the "great men of faith" in Hebrews chapter 11.

† Why do you think she was chosen to be numbered here instead of women like Ruth or Esther?
† How does she express her faith in the incident with the spies?
† Would you say that reading and hearing about the ways in which God works in people's lives inspires faith in you?

REFLECTION

† Rahab's home was built into the city wall. Think for a moment about where you live. What kind of area do you live in and what kind of people do you live near?
† List ways in which you think the place where you live could be used strategically for God's work in helping to bring peace, justice and salvation to others. What might this involve? List possible pros and cons.

There may be one or two people in the group who would like to share what they have written with the group as a whole. You might also like to keep your thoughts in a notebook and update it from time to time as your experience and understanding change.

WORSHIP

Turn what you have written into a prayer or meditation, thanking God for all the adventures that are possible when we offer him what he has given us, and put our faith in him to use it for his purposes. Be honest about your hopes and fears as you consider what God may be requiring of you.

List things which may make it particularly difficult for you to live with what God wants you to do. Ask him to work in those areas, and to bring you the resources and encouragement that you need.

SESSION FOUR

THE HOME: A PLACE OF DEFIANCE AND OBEDIENCE

" **A** candle-light is a protest at midnight.
It is a non-conformist.
It says to the darkness,
'I beg to differ'." *Samuel Reyan*

AIM

The aim of this session is to recognize the importance of living according to God's principles, whoever might try and persuade you to do otherwise. Our homes can become places where either loved ones or strangers can tempt us to disregard what we know to be right. This can happen in all kinds of different ways. Our home, a place of safety and delight, can suddenly become the very place where decisions we make can suddenly turn it into a place full of regrets. Being aware of this is not meant to make you afraid or anxious. Rather, by studying God's Word and allowing it to permeate our whole life, we can build up inner strength which will help us say "no" to what we know to be wrong, and "yes" to everything that leads to life, health and peace.

TO TALK ABOUT

You discover that your partner or close friend has been

running up serious debts. You don't know what the money has been spent on, but over dinner one evening he or she asks you if you could lend him or her a large sum of money. What is your immediate response?

Turn to the person next to you and tell them what you would say and how you would handle the situation.

† Think about compromising situations you have found yourself in. What are the main issues at stake?
† On what basis have you made your decisions in such circumstances? Were they rational or intuitive decisions? Were they based on principle, or maybe out of fear, or were you simply swept along by the situation at hand?
† How have you dealt with compromising situations when afterwards you knew you had made a mistake?
† Have these situations occurred when you have been on your own, or with other people in your household? What difference, if any, has that made?
† What advice would you give to someone whom you know is about to get involved in a compromising situation, or do you think it's not your business to interfere?

DEFIANCE AND OBEDIENCE

The following passage comes from the book of Exodus. It tells the story of two Hebrew midwives. These women disobeyed the king's orders when he told them to kill every new-born boy in order to secure his own position. Although this was an extreme situation, the Hebrew midwives, along with the rest of their people, were still slaves in Egypt. They didn't have any power or influence. Their decision to defy the king could easily have cost them their lives. Yet because they feared God and acted upon his principles in difficult circumstances, God honoured them. As we shall see, this

20

had wonderful consequences, both immediately and long term.

Read the passage now.

15Then the king of Egypt spoke to Shiphrah and Puah, the two midwives who helped the Hebrew women. 16"When you help the Hebrew women give birth," he said to them, "kill the baby if it is a boy; but if it is a girl, let it live." 17But the midwives feared God and so did not obey the king; instead, they let the boys live. 18So the king sent for the midwives and asked them, "Why are you doing this? Why are you letting the boys live?"

19They answered, "The Hebrew women are not like Egyptian women; they give birth easily, and their babies are born before either of us gets there." 20–21Because the midwives feared God, he was good to them and gave them families of their own. And the Israelites continued to increase and become strong.

Exodus 1.15–21

DIGGING DEEPER

† Do you think the Hebrew midwives understood the king's motives? Did it matter?

† What does this say to us when we find ourselves in situations which require compromise, or a deliberate going against God's Word?

† How did the midwives justify their actions? Were they being honest?

† Is there ever a situation where bending or concealing the truth is better than presenting a situation straight? If so, give an example.

Now read this passage:

During this time a man from the tribe of Levi married a woman of his own tribe, 2and she bore him a son. When she saw what a fine baby he was, she hid him for three months. 3But when she could not hide him any longer, she took a basket made of reeds and covered it

21

with tar to make it watertight. She put the baby in it and then placed it in the tall grass at the edge of the river. ⁴The baby's sister stood some distance away to see what would happen to him.

⁵The king's daughter came down to the river to bathe, while her servants walked along the bank. Suddenly she noticed the basket in the tall grass and sent a slave-girl to get *it. ⁶The princess opened it and saw a baby boy. He was crying, and she felt sorry for him. "This is one of the Hebrew babies," she said.*

⁷Then his sister asked her, "Shall I go and call a Hebrew woman to act as a wet-nurse?"

⁸"Please do," she answered. So the girl went and brought the baby's own mother.

Exodus 2.1–8

† How does this passage relate to women today who, through no fault of their own, don't have access to their children?

† What can be learned from the behaviour of the Hebrew women here?

† How would you attempt to help a woman trying to regain access to her child, if legally she had every right to do so?

Re-read the passage, and apply the symbols to what you have read.

 something you have learned about God

 something you have learned about yourself or human nature

 a new insight

 something to put into practice

 something to do together

REFLECTION

Read and meditate on this poem by Ulrich Schaeffer.

I am persuaded by the dandelion
to take the wings of the updrift
to parachute into enemy country
to fall to the ground
to be walked on
to lose beauty
to die
and so to give birth
to a whole new generation of flyers

† How can this be true in your own life: now and in the future? Write down what prevents this from becoming a reality in your life.

WORSHIP

Turn what you have written into a prayer and ask the Holy Spirit to work through these things with you.

Turn to the person next to you and each share something from what you have discovered about yourself, and pray for each other. Date your prayer and watch for God to work in your life.

SESSION FIVE

THE HOME OF THE COMMITTED WOMAN: A PLACE OF HONOUR AND INFLUENCE

"The will-o-the-wisp, end-of-the-rainbow, daydream idea of happiness: happy marriages, happy families, and 'having a right to happiness', doesn't touch upon reality. What is a family? It is a blending of people for whom a career of making a shelter in the time of storm is worth a lifetime!" *Edith Schaeffer*

AIM

The aim of this study is to explore how any woman with a real Christian commitment can make her home a place of honour and influence. The passage talks in traditional terms about the capable wife, but is as applicable to single mothers and women who are not married, or who live alone.

TO TALK ABOUT

† Imagine you are at a party or having coffee with a group of friends. Someone asks you what job you do. How would you reply?

† Turn to the person next to you, and in a couple of minutes tell him or her about your home, who lives there with you, and what "home" means to you. Swap roles and repeat the exercise.

† What do you think makes an ideal home?

1. the building itself and the ways it's decorated
2. the relationships between those who live there
3. when Mum waits on everyone
4. a place where you can relax and invite people round, no matter how big or small it may be.

Choose one or two of the above, turn to someone near you and discuss.

† What different pictures of "home" are represented in the group? Ask two or three people to share their "homes" with the rest of the group. What main features emerge?

HONOUR AND INFLUENCE

The passage below celebrates the virtues of the capable wife. For many women it is a thoroughly depressing picture: a stereotype of today's Superwoman which most women, whether married or not, feel they could never live up to.

¹⁰*How hard it is to find a capable wife! She is worth far more than jewels!*

¹¹*Her husband puts his confidence in her, and he will never be poor.*

¹²*As long as she lives, she does him good and never harm.*

¹³*She keeps herself busy making wool and linen cloth.*

¹⁴*She brings home food from out-of-the-way places, as merchant ships do.*

¹⁵*She gets up before daylight to prepare food for her family and to tell her servant-girls what to do.*

¹⁶*She looks at land and buys it, and with money she has earned she plants a vineyard.*

¹⁷*She is a hard worker, strong and industrious.*

¹⁸*She knows the value of everything she makes, and works late into the night.*

¹⁹*She spins her own thread and weaves her own cloth.*

²⁰*She is generous to the poor and needy.*

²¹*She doesn't worry when it snows, because her family has warm clothing.*

²²*She makes bedspreads and*

wears clothes of fine purple linen.
²³Her husband is well known, one of the leading citizens. ²⁴She makes clothes and belts, and sells them to merchants. ²⁵She is strong and respected and not afraid of the future. ²⁶She speaks with a gentle wisdom. ²⁷She is always busy and looks after her family's needs. ²⁸Her children show their appreciation, and her husband praises her. ²⁹He says, "Many women are good wives, but you are the best of them all." ³⁰Charm is deceptive and beauty disappears, but a woman who honours the LORD should be praised. ³¹Give her credit for all she does. She deserves the respect of everyone.

Proverbs 31.10–31

DIGGING DEEPER

† What is your immediate reaction to this passage?

† In general terms, how is it relevant to women in the home today?

† List the verses which place this picture into the culture of its time (e.g. verse 15: "she gets up before daylight to make food for her family and tell her servant girls what to do.")

† Now list those verses which could be as easily relevant today. Which verses do you feel are most relevant to you? – both those you can identify with in your present situation, and those which challenge you to adopt more biblical principles in your home and the way you use it.

Now read this passage.

Timothy, Paul and Silas are on a missionary journey, and arrive in Philippi. Here they find a place by the riverside which they thought would be a place of prayer. They get into conversation with a group of women, one of whom is Lydia.

¹⁴One of those who heard us was Lydia from Thyatira, who was a dealer in purple cloth. She was a woman who worshipped God, and

the Lord opened her mind to pay attention to what Paul was saying. [15] After she and the people of her house had been baptized, she invited us. "Come and stay in my house if you have decided that I am a true believer in the Lord." And she persuaded us to go.

Acts 16.14–15

† Notice how Lydia's whole household was baptized. What does this passage say to Christian women who live with people who are not Christians?

† What guidelines would you give to the following people about offering hospitality to visiting preachers and missionaries?

1. single women sharing a house or living alone
2. single female parents with children
3. married women with families
4. older widows living alone

Ask a woman in the group to talk about how she has used her home effectively to extend hospitality to others.

Re-read the passage, and apply the symbols to what you have read.

 something you have learned about God

 something you have learned about yourself or human nature

 a new insight

 something to put into practice

 something to do together

REFLECTION

✝ Think about the home you grew up in. Write down what you valued most about it. Now write down what you found most difficult. How is your own home different?

✝ Write a letter to either or both your parents if they are still alive, and thank them for what you genuinely appreciated about the home they provided for you.

WORSHIP

"A family – for better or for worse, for richer for poorer, in sickness and in health. Dirty nappies, chicken pox, broken dishes, scratched furniture, arguments; laughter and tears. For all this and much more we thank you God. For even in the biggest muddle and the most heated conflicts, you are with us helping us to put together the broken pieces, to say sorry: to start again – this is how real homes are made."
Edith Schaeffer

Remember your parents and those who grew up with you.

Pray for each in turn, thanking God for all that was good in your relationships together.
Write on a piece of paper anything you feel you still haven't forgiven, or are not able to forgive, members of your family for.
Ask God to help you. Maybe this will involve seeking appropriate counselling. Ask the group leader for advice if you think this may be the case.

SESSION SIX

THE HOME: A PLACE OF MIRACLES AND HEALING

"The Lord's goodness surrounds us at every moment, I walk through it almost with difficulty, as through thick grass and flowers." *R W Barbour*

AIM

The aim of this session is to see how God can be active in our homes through healing and miracles. While there may be those in the group who have prayed for the healing of a loved one which has not taken place, the point here is to stress how God honours those who live life his way, often rewarding those who do so in the most unexpected and wonderful ways.

TO TALK ABOUT

† Someone in your family has a long term illness. How would this affect your understanding of God's love? Turn to the person next to you and talk about it.

† Imagine you are on the popular radio programme "Just a Minute". You are asked to speak for one minute on the subject of "miracles". How would you tackle it? Take a moment to think about this, then ask for one volunteer. What were some of the main points that were made? As many people as possible should comment.

MIRACLES AND HEALING

The following passage takes us into the homes of Dorcas and the little sick girl. Read the passage either individually or together.

³⁶*In Joppa there was a woman named Tabitha, who was a believer. (Her name in Greek is Dorcas, meaning "a deer".) She spent all her time doing good and helping the poor. ³⁷At that time she became ill and died. Her body was washed and laid in a room upstairs. ³⁸Joppa was not very far from Lydda, and when the believers in Joppa heard that Peter was in Lydda, they sent two men to him with the message, "Please hurry and come to us." ³⁹So Peter got ready and went with them. When he arrived, he was taken to the room upstairs, where all the widows crowded round him, crying and showing him all the shirts and coats that Dorcas had made while she was alive. ⁴⁰Peter put them all out of the room, and knelt down and prayed; then he turned to the body and said, "Tabitha, get up!" She opened her eyes, and when she saw Peter, she sat up. ⁴¹Peter reached over and helped her get up. Then he called all the believers, including the widows, and presented her alive to them. ⁴²The news about this spread all over Joppa, and many people believed in the Lord.*

Acts 9.36–42

† What an extraordinary scene! Imagine you were there when this happened. Get into groups of three, and number yourselves one to three. Now describe how you would have reacted:

1. If you had been Peter
2. If you had been one of the widows
3. If you had been Dorcas

† What does the passage tell us about death and mourning in the culture in which it was written?

† What do you think is being said in verses 39 and 40?

. † What can we learn from verse 42 when we think of our responsibility to tell others about how God is active in our lives? Does the media have a place here?

Now read this passage, which is the story of the healing of Jairus' daughter.

⁴⁹*While Jesus was saying this, a messenger came from the official's house. "Your daughter has died," he told Jairus; "don't bother the Teacher any longer."*

⁵⁰*But Jesus heard it and said to Jairus, "Don't be afraid; only believe, and she will be well."*

⁵¹*When he arrived at the house, he would not let anyone go in with him except Peter, John, and James, and the child's father and mother.* ⁵²*Everyone there was crying and mourning for the child. Jesus said,*

"Don't cry; the child is not dead – she is only sleeping!"

⁵³*They all laughed at him, because they knew that she was dead.* ⁵⁴*But Jesus took her by the hand and called out, "Get up, my child!"* ⁵⁵*Her life returned, and she got up at once, and Jesus ordered them to give her something to eat.* ⁵⁶*Her parents were astounded, but Jesus commanded them not to tell anyone what had happened.*

Luke 8.49–56

DIGGING DEEPER

† What strikes you most about this story in comparison to the previous one? What similarities do they have? How are they different?

† What do you think Jesus meant in verse 52?

† Why do you think he told the little girl's parents not to tell anyone? (Verse 56).

Re-read the passages, and apply the symbols to what you have read.

 something you have learned about God

 something you have learned about yourself or human nature

 a new insight

31

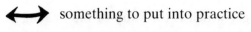 something to put into practice

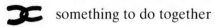 something to do together

REFLECTION

"And still I rise." *Maya Angelou*

† In what ways has God shown his love to you when a member of your family has been sick at home?
† What other ways has God surprised you by giving you unexpected miracles and healing through your home?

WORSHIP

Thank God for the ways in which he has helped you and been real to you in your life, especially through difficult times. Pray for all who are homeless and who fail to see God at work in their lives.

As you approach the end of these studies, meditate on the following poem, which portrays God as a weaver, creating unique and beautiful garments out of the rough fabric of our lives.

Not until the loom is silent,
and the shuttles cease to fly,
Will God unroll the canvas,
and explain the reasons why;
How the dark threads are as needful
in the weaver's skilful hand,
As the threads of gold and silver,
in the pattern he has planned.
Author unknown.